as she appears

as she appears

yesyes books · portland

shelley wong

AS SHE APPEARS © 2022 BY SHELLEY WONG

PROJECT EDITOR: STEVIE EDWARDS

COVER & INTERIOR DESIGN: ALBAN FISCHER

ISBN 978-1-936919-89-5

PUBLISHED BY YESYES BOOKS

1631 NE BROADWAY ST #121

PORTLAND, OR 97232

YESYESBOOKS.COM

KMA SULLIVAN, PUBLISHER

STEVIE EDWARDS, SENIOR EDITOR, BOOK DEVELOPMENT

ALBAN FISCHER, GRAPHIC DESIGNER

COLE HILDEBRAND, MANAGING EDITOR

ALEXIS SMITHERS, ASSISTANT EDITOR

AMBER RAMBHAROSE, ASSISTANT EDITOR, INSTAGRAM

JAMES SULLIVAN, ASSISTANT EDITOR, AUDIO BOOKS

PHILLIP B. WILLIAMS, COEDITOR IN CHIEF, *VINYL*

AMIE ZIMMERMAN, EVENTS COORDINATOR

for the quiet sisters

Contents

Yes, we had heard music together
Yes, we had gone to the sea together

. . . .

Yes, it was beginning in each
Yes, it threw waves across our lives

. . . .

Yes, we were looking at each other

—Muriel Rukeyser

//

For the Living in the New World

There are so many ways to explore a forest—
over clover clusters, past skunk cabbages

to a field where we listen for a ghost
of song. The hypergreen periphery

is the opposite of Los Angeles on fire.
Any tree can become a ladder. These trees have

too many branches, but it is not my place
to revise them. I may be happiest

improvising the language a body can make
on a dance floor. We are just learning

how female birds sing in the tropics.
Spring insists we can build the world

around us again. How has love brought you
here? My head is heavy from the crown.

Private Collection

At the San Francisco Museum of Modern Art
the ocean drawn in pencil is no longer
on display. I once thought *I could wreck*
that water. My partner liked a painting

of a blonde woman reading a newspaper,
a sister to a Dutch painting I admired
back in New York, where a woman
contemplates a water pitcher

in cathedral light. We walked gallery to gallery
& no women resembled us. I'm charmed
by certain French words, but forget what they mean
& never properly pronounce them—

mélange, de rigueur, au courant. Sometimes
couples become echoes of one another.
We wore quiet glasses, our hair in low ponytails
like George Washington. She would photograph me

when I looked away from her, as I glanced
at the curves of the Grand Tetons, the raised head
of the Greek caryatid locked in the British Museum,
a winter forest floor

somewhere in Oregon when we were nineteen
& I couldn't meet the camera's gaze,
    though I knew she was there & that she
        would hold me from a distance.

Department of the Interior

The tide calls the water
of the body. Fire Island spans 32 miles
                   & is drifting west. A maze
cuts through the salt marsh, bridging bay
                   to ocean. Where I wander
is federal land, not a branched
                   interlude of neon pool parties.
I'm part of the sky paparazzi
                   dazed by its flaring—*rainbow, rainbow, rainbow!*
Stumbling in the sand, I find only
                   the crash of return. I have come to this
barrier island again, in the silence that follows
                   a separation. Tomorrow
there will be three boats
                   at various distances. One jet-ski.
Lightning like a rumor of another realm.
                   I try to divide eleven years, but cannot be held
to exactness. My mind floats out to water
                   & I am living through this world once.

To Yellow

Your orb over the Pacific
casts a glittering runway.

You are unfairly suspect—as *peril*, a *fever*—
though you are as chill

as lemonade, dangling from trees
with the ease of a summer

spent on a porch swing. Ladies
make linen A-line dresses

out of pineapple print, reclining
in your sun though it blinds

& burns them. Dear yellow, you
have never covered my body.

I leave your light in the dark.
At seventeen, I saw a film

where the heartbreaker girl
only wore green so my colors

turned verdant. When you appear
on the face of books, I ask *why*

is it always you? Last spring
I bought a yellow purse

& hope that it will turn heavy
with gold. I am still learning to hold

certain illuminations, like how quiet
is strong & often beautiful.

No longer green, I write you
to learn your minor keys. My people

are rising. We are the new names,
the ones we have always known.

Women After Midnight

The red minute hand insists we sleep
or commit to our rendezvous. On a deserted street
a woman exits the opera house
parading toward me in a single

long shot. *Tick tock.* It's our secret.
Who is calling at this hour? A dark-haired man
kisses Michelle Pfeiffer's spine with precision
in digital clock light. Another man

deletes a gagged woman
from the frame. The camera
says nothing. In black & white time
women sleep with painted lips

clasped shut like purses.
A lamp comes on. *For god's sake,*
it's 2 AM. Brigitte Bardot enters the kitchen
still clad in her red bustier gown

& drains the milk. A girl stumbles
down a spiral staircase, fleeing from shadows
in the piano dark. A girl wakes up
when my hands clench her neck

as if it were a bell rope.
She flails for the baseball bat, but this
is her dream at 2:18. Slick stilettos
come off first. A woman hangs

up the phone & lies in bed
like a floral question mark. The ferry departs
on the half hour. *You're so pretty*
when you sleep.

Dear Frida

You have me tangled
in flower names. Skulls chatter
as I tango with a woman

or a man. We are twinned.
I imagine us on a patio above the sea—
you with your tequila & me

with my Martinelli's cider
chortling at those who click
their tongues at us. You turn

my hand over in yours
as I tell you how I prayed
for the flood. We're not ghosts—

who isn't lonely?
He approves of your dresses
when your skirts unfurl

into a temple. Let the parrots loose
when you hear his fist against
your locked door. I was once

caught in my own silence,
that sharp circle. To call
my lover away from

her grief, her desperate
wandering: I undid
my departures. Lived

in a quiet interior, waking
with my light elsewhere,
scattered across the waves.

Perennials

Once she named them—Hong Kong orchids—
the voluptuous pink blossoms were everywhere.

Without her, I find they are the first
flowers to open in the Columbus Park of Roses.

They bloom like an aria. The rose plots
are just woodchips, slashed stems, & thorns.

Years ago, we lived on a city island where she could
barely breathe because the Norway maple trees

cast their pollen like ticker tape & we
wanted to keep the cats. Freely, she spoke,

being proudly out, while I feared cruelty
& broke my meaning. How dazzling when trees

burst into glamour, flowers releasing
into symmetry. She lives on a foggy

peninsula & I hear she's smoking
again. I see the spring as a closing throat.

White Rabbit

When I sit before the empty frame, I face a man. We are the audience
as the Alices come between us. They lie back against each other like pages,
blue touching blue. The dark-haired one approaches me, intent, almost writhing,
but looks beyond, moving like a ribbon & staring off at something unnameable.

In the office, we paint roses harlot red. The White Rabbit crawls
across cabinets & swings the lamp *tick tock, tick tock.* He exits & shuts me in—
my cue to leap & open drawers: locked, locked, white rose, white rose—

At his desk, Lewis says, "*You have split me in two*"... *are you getting this?*
I peer down at my ink swirls & scratches. Yes, I say, because I am loath
to ruin illusions. Before we dress up, the Mad Hatter asks about
my history of analysis. I play my part as if I'm clean as an apron. *Not all hatters
are mad, you know. How is a writing desk like a raven?* she asks.
Feathers, I reply, & it is her turn to be silent.

Lewis & Alice sway in the stairwell. She walks the banister & collapses
into his arms again & again like the stumbling of the resolute
or the damned. We watch, caught in the steps, suspended in a threshold—

The Summer Forecast

Is it too late to go off-
the-shoulder?

Linen jumpsuits
leapt over me

as I cut pastel flowers
off Highway 1:

whisper pink, lavender,
spiked butter.

I wore a long, striped dress,
a sailor ashore

longing to be
a natural wonder.

I take a page
& sew by hand—

piercing, piercing
then rip out & realign

bringing me to think
of Penelope unraveling,

coiling her colors back
like a bad tide

after another day
untouched. But I am

no lady-in-waiting.
I gather the bouquet

myself. Don't sleep
on peonies, their

intricate unfolding,
whirling faces.

I felt the cold
weight in my hand

as I approached
softness with shears.

//

Walking Across Fire Island

The ocean crashes & the bay rolls in.
Planks creak along the boardwalk
as a deer emerges. Umbrellas open
like sudden fruit, while I inhale salt air,
the fog that lifts off the brush. Here, I can let
the deer know me. The daytrippers have sailed
& the sun is falling. A woman once said
deer are dumb. Deer or gentle friend
or mothering question, perpetual guest,
Long Island duchess, beach hostess.
I am in a floating year. They must all be
related by now, the deer, like beaches.
I imagine a deer stepping out of the ocean
as water returns to me, rushing over my hands.

Refrain

Farewell, romantic
sacrifice:

I choose myself.
Some can only

love once.
How true

will it be? I love
sequins, but get

the sequence
confused.

At our end, I broke
from her

& every face grew
stranger. Stranger,

speak to me
like light

through a veil.
Like a spent match

the darlings
turn to find me

& I fade
into the glitter.

A sequoia has
every vowel.

Every vow
like a closed hand.

When I've worn
my body down

from dancing, I still
point to the sky.

I will honor
my body, my only.

My only body,
its honor, my will.

Memorial Day Weekend

On Fire Island: elevated pine houses in case of flooding

    The shoulder season is for lovers

        It is the first weekend to wear white, eggshell, ecru, pearl

    Leaves of three along the boardwalk call out for libidinal chaos

        I collect light from every window

A scattered puzzle mixes sky & ocean, sand & stone

    The light alone a majesty

        To dwell in a maritime forest away from the seductions

    Recording the tide's hiss, water lapping, a catbird wheezing

        The ferryman asks *where are you from* & I answer *California* & tip well

To be given the sister ocean—the dark Atlantic—where all of our streets once ended

    A temporary expanse, a cold, hypnotic blue

        Eating bulgogi with kimchi & rice on the deck

To wake at dawn madly scratching, the body an alarm

        Mosquito girls flying with my spiced blood

All Beyoncés & Lucy Lius

where are you from / the LBC /
can you speak / har gow siu mai /

I am four generations
deep / in America / dial up

the boba to 75% sweetness
50% ice / what do your people

call jook / Chinese people
skip the fourth floor /

don't trust a pho place
without a number in its name /

enter June Lena Rose & Waverly /
enter Lucy Liu & my girl Drew /

lucky white ceramic cats
collect what's owed / Hello Kitty

Little Twin Stars My Melody /
did you know Keanu Reeves

is part Chinese / his Hawaiian name means
cool breeze over the mountains /

the most exquisite loneliness
is Maggie Cheung gliding in a cheongsam

as she ascends a staircase /
in my domestic dress

I calculate my proportions with finesse /
Like a G6 / tell me the best

midnight restaurant in Chinatown /
we run with the yellow

Power Ranger / eat turkey jook
after Thanksgiving / enter Claudia Kishi

licking salt off her fingers /
did you watch Keanu & River Phoenix

in My Own Private Idaho / is my eyeliner
even / I can't tell Mandarin

from Cantonese / drink hot water
to flush the fat / how did Michelle Kwan

change you / Fields of Gold
forever / Mulan against the world /

are you wearing black tonight / Cibo Matto
is playing at the Bronze /

Chinese love cash /
little girls dressed in pink & red

Exit Strategist

A quarrel in white.

                                    In noir low light, the women

don't know who to turn to. Veil of splitting leaves

                                    veil soaked in rosé

fluorescent veil

                                    for kicks. Pine tree shadows

approach. You're my witness.

                                    The dirty perfume we trample.

Stacked baskets

                                    with too many arrows.

My sword

                                    crossed yours. I win, I win.

Don't touch the trees

                                    don't clap three times. All the pretty moths

represent. One bird, one way out.

                                        Is this a game?

Broken bridge

                        says the bannerman. I hold a dead lighter

& the good book of knots.

                                        Like a long apple peel

she goes by. These arts I invented

                                        so he could not refuse me.

A bowl full of fish

                                        writhing in place. Out over the water

I walk the plank, I'm off

                                        this ship—

Watch Hill

We drift over the dunes to the swales,
forest & salt marsh, reaching the bay
in less than a mile. Along a jagged pine path,
I walk with Ranger Kelsey, who loves
the sassafras tree for its soft leaves
of one, two, & three lobes like paw prints
or a child's looped sketch. The tide breaks
in a slow echo as they explain
how salt prunes the treetops. I ask about
the thin, curved trees leaning at various
angles around us, which I privately name
the queer trees for their arcs & intertwining.
They have three names: *Juneberry* for timing,
the shad tree for blooming when the fish
are biting, & *service berry* for emerging when
all the ice has melted back into the earth
so we can dig & bury our dead.
Kelsey distinguishes non-native plants
from invasive species, as some are
from elsewhere, but aren't overgrowing.
Two white-tailed does sip fresh water
at the pond. There are too many deer
on the island as they have no natural
predators & tourists keep feeding them.
The does eye us & turn back into the tall grass.

Did you see all the ticks on their faces?
they ask & I flinch. We see the grass shift
& laugh at their languorous retreat.
A sour smell rises & Kelsey spots
a crushed deer carcass. I don't say
how yesterday I came across a fawn
near the body. *Its child,* I imagined.
Kelsey tells tourists about wild blueberries
before & after they ripen—their own
private sweetness. They say dirty water
is healthy water & that the woodpecker
is careful to leave gaps between holes
to keep a tree alive. While we sleep,
horseshoe crabs emerge along the shore,
older than dinosaurs. Another tide cuts through:
after a hurricane, one island breach remains
for the ocean to renew the bay.

Pride Month

"It is June. I am tired of being brave."
—Anne Sexton

It is June & I read about having grace to forgive those
who would condemn us. It is June & a man reads a poem
where the father becomes a dying stag & the son says
there is something I need to tell you. It was June when I was
awake past midnight gathering news about the Pulse
nightclub shooting. I fell asleep knowing I would wake
to walk against grief in waves. It is June & I am happy
that Tegan & Sara will appear in San Francisco
or Oakland. It is June & I have never prayed to any god.
It was New York in the 2000s when my ex ran
the chaos backstage at the Pride pier dance.
In strobing summer heat, we slid through a sea of men
with shaved chests. The songs hardly had words
& the bass shuddered into our bodies. Fireworks climaxed
over the Hudson & the crowd rocked & roared back.
I stood in a tropical sundress in the VIP section
surrounded by so many barely dressed people double-
kissing my face saying *happy Pride & where is your wife?*

Weather Advisory

it is foggy & the ferry will not travel east—the captain lost
without his radar sonar—*excuse me sirs this is a gay*

dancing emergency—is heterosexuality the fog—I am slow
with too much time, dressed in four shades of grey

& a streak of pink—oh it's an older crowd—
oh that's me—we all had the same Madonna-Whitney childhood

set to synthesizer beats—today I tried to pluck a pinecone
but the stem said no—*I am sorry, tree, I meant*

to ask consent—between the Pines & Cherry Grove,
there is one path for tourists, another for cruising—

among the rangers, I feel famous (*are you*
the writer)—*hello bird*—I have no sweetness

to offer the bees—where did Frank O'Hara wander
& fall asleep on the beach—the first inhabitant of Fire Island

was a shipwrecker—he lured ships to shore
& killed the crews—it is not certain

whether the island is named for these warning flames
or its sunsets—*I am a fire sign—who should I touch*

with this burning—I loop along the bay—
the marina—the beach—emptied of families—

in the straight neighborhood, I watch men on break
pause one by one to take in my neon floral shorts

they reveal my kiss of a birthmark—the walk
of a messy-haired woman—some faraway flower

The Fall Forecast

Every autumn, editors name the leaves anew:
burgundy, emerald, bronze, chartreuse.
They want women to wear Europe,
gemstone, antique metal steeped in liqueur
exclusively made by monks. It takes
a strong woman to wear bejeweled armor
& traipse through Germany
slightly buzzed.
                    This season,
the must-have mineral is rutilated quartz:
its embedded crystal needles
mimic gold or rust. Such flaws
are forgiven.
                    If the line looks familiar,
consider Chanel who said *creativity*
is the act of concealing your sources.
Boom. The recent is always
losing luster.
                    Perhaps the decaying leaf
is the new beauty. When they say you're only as good
as your last collection, one considers trends.
Use bold text for counterpoint, stranger danger.
Open the floor if the show becomes too
matchy-matchy.

Editors caress
rough edges & think *how fin de siècle.*
Models dishevel in layers, cracking leather
under the lights.
The girls look like night trees.

//

Monolids

In the ghostly movie palace
our eyes weep at our eyes
elated across the screen. Biggest

little eyes. We are alive
& ancient. Our eyes
soften our eyes, clean

or dressed in glitter
& smoke. Our gaze facets
kaleidoscopic. Our eyes

are next-door eyes
but sometimes our eyes
want to stay unread.

Two women
glance at each other
in a field & no one

says *sanctuary* or *belonging.*
Tonight, the silver storm
shakes like a hologram

as we trace fires burning
along the opposite shore.
Our eyes close, but do not

go out. Our eyes illuminate
our gathering, collide
reaching for our eyes.

Epithalamium

to Frida Kahlo

Lady, keep the tequila
by your lamp for when
you need a knife.

Dip the brush in azul
for feathers so a bird
will fly above your bed

& you can wash away
the memory of his sweat,
the drowning taste

of chandeliered women.
Always, you are twinned:
one side a mirror, the other

a window—you have already
changed the sky. Girls are
stripping the petals, dusting

their mouths with sugar
& smashed pecans.
When you spin

in your white dress,
greet the crowd with your
stained mouth. A *dove*

& an elephant, they
murmur, but you're
rewriting the song

into a jungle. Bring out
the longest rope & tie it
to him—say *I will look at you*

until the blood runs out.
This is when shadows
start & you will walk him

back to the banquet,
knowing that what is white
is not innocent, nor safe.

The Ocean Will Take Us One Day

A supermoon opened
its brightness. My first memory

is when the tide pulled me

into its room. The last time
the moon aligned so close to earth

was the year my mother

came into being. On land I can still lose
my boundary, identifying

with the ocean & not the lake.

When you enter a city, check the elevation
on the welcome sign.

We saw over 300 Native tribes

gather in North Dakota
to protect a river. Saw the river

transgressed: the police shooting water cannons

in freezing weather.
Was it worth it, what you did

to live by the sea? Stay with me

in bare light, undone.
In recovery, two states

drift toward one another

& repel, like soldiers. Rapture, yes
I've felt that, too. Who will stop a man

from having his way? Breathless, a woman

rests her head on her longtime companion
as they listen to the waves.

Invitation with Three Colors

It's come to this:
I want the arrow

between us.
My dear,

what do you
know of blood?

I forget—
& don't dream.

My haunting:
spring

in abeyance.
A black-tie hunter

& the un-
startled prey:

we fall away
from each other

like cut flowers.
You drag back

the trigger,
the knifed stem

as I pull the bow.

The Allergy Test

The doctor said *you wear black*
  well, but you might consider
   changing your wardrobe.
    My closet clutched herself.
     In this life, I hold on to what
      echoes my body, what marks me
       as one of my people. I don't wear black
        to mourn. I armor myself
         against a world that makes me itch.
          I want to believe love is where
          I am safe in my own mind
           & body. To let go of pain
            as an anchor. There is a look
             to every exchange, a kind of weather.

Vermeer at the Metropolitan Museum of Art

At her toilette, the young woman does not ask
for our devotion. Ultramarine edges her linen

& we hear the sea slap against ships.
Her braided bodice is articulated

like the stained-glass window that lets light
enter in many directions, keeping us

gazing in. The scene is cast & re-cast
as if it were lapis lazuli

refracting. She lifts the window,
steadies the water pitcher & her arms

are a bridge. Is the map a reminder
or a wish? The answer for where

we are meant to wander won't be
unveiled praying to paint. Her face

is a mirror that looks away from us.

Interlude

Walking through
the hills, I heard leaves
break & through
an enclosed fence
I saw a fawn pacing
uphill toward me.
As it skittered &
turned, I heard
no other companions.
The fence was locked
so I whispered *go*
back as it darted
like a child
uncertain whether
to disobey. It descended
to the path below
where the buildings
were closely plotted
& dark. *What happened*
to its mother, I wondered
as the cars passed
behind me, heading
deeper into the hills.
Then the fawn returned
& retreated, in a repeat

like a pas de bourrée
seeing the lit park
beyond. I took a photo
& blinked, having
set its distress
aside for beauty.
An *unmotherly instinct*
I thought, *for a not-*
mother.

Albino

The white peacock is in love
& is all that I see. Dear
Spanish fan, immaculate flutter.
His feathers undulate & ask
to be touched. Soft prince,
how your careful blankness
staggers. The world defines itself
by your plumed horizon. He preens
in the dirt, struck by two peahens
with cream-colored breasts
& cerulean throats, their feathers
gathered like brown arrows.
He flirts his white crown & sways
his doily array, but the ladies are busy
with an itch. My trademark move:
unpinning my highest hair.
Look at me, he blooms, pivoting
to display his beating wings.
In the end, I will say
that I, too, worshipped beauty,
parading in my pastels.
I fought & loved the silences.

The Winter Forecast

this open interval: when nightgowns glow & stalk the field

in Chinese, two trees make a forest

as an inoculation against loneliness, models hold hands, clutch collarless coats

who is she & where is she going—her outfit as consequence

in French, the ocean is masculine, the sea feminine

how does a rhyme determine fate: daughter // laughter // slaughter

two ways to survive: analog & digital

we can hear tree rings rendered as sound

diamonds shine in icicles, in a spidering necklace

aboard the single swan boat, she cries *not the underworld!*

jump out of your big sister, matroyshka

for the encore, the cashmered girls sleep with velvet eyes

a finger to their lips: no trespassing on the runway

women in black embroider orchids in the orchestra pit

//

One seems to be able to see her. One imagines her, already.
—Theresa Hak Kyung Cha

Winter Pineapple with Sea

When the sun pierces
my brick turret, I awaken

with drawn-out limbs,
a spare dancer, dreamless

in a beam of dust.
What's in my chest

is not a fist, nor a peony
but something

knotted & harder
to pull awake. I sense

its shooting music
& not its heat.

Like a returning sea
captain, I should

place a pineapple
by the door

as an invitation
for guests. Down

the street, a tree
strips to bone.

Because she peeled
my first peach, they rot

in my kitchen. I keep
buying them, though

the thought
of their sweetness

stings. In the polar
winter, snow

erases snow.
I leap over ice

in a pineapple skirt
as the wind sends

its voltage through
the low landscape.

I see
& tell myself

I am seeing.
Startle, startle

I say, a hand
on my heart.

How the season holds,
rippling arpeggios

while I play
a spectator,

a flash of gold,
a ship dropped

in a stilled sea.

Courtship

Instead of emojis, bring out the paper fans.
If I hold the spread fan with the right hand

in front of my face, I mean *follow me.*
Sometimes a trapeze does an extra swing

or two while I steady
my yes-no smile. Hey young man

don't shake the fire tree if you shiver
at sparks. I have one silver tooth

& the rest is bone. My skirts
are tidal. I want to enter the Pure Gold

Restoration Clinic by instinct
but lack the treasure. I try on crowns

because I walk the walk. With age
we learn the lines of our bodies.

Don't tell me what's unbecoming
for a woman: I was raised on magazines.

All trends wheel around.
I can't say why the world

is so broken, caught
in a tunneling scream. Still, I aspire

to be kissed by the sun. Exalt
all women. I'm the tree coming back

through the page. If I'm honest,
most mornings my skeleton

aches a little. If I unfold
the fan slowly, wait for me.

My Therapist Asks If I Would Be Happier If I Were Straight

I have trees in my mind
& rivers too.

Drown the world
that gives us two Xs

for our eyes. With
the right song, I'll dance

down my bones.
I use a trapdoor

when I erase my feeling.
When I take cover

I forgive myself.
These days, I'm

busy stitching
my breath. Desire

becomes a distant edge.
As a girl, I never

saw a woman
who looked like me.

I had to invent her.
I'm inventing her.

Pursuit

What did you buy for me
in Connecticut? A *small,*
strange gift, you wrote.
We met at a lakeside retreat.
You were perpetually emo
with a voice like a struck
match. In your black t-shirt
you would lose your sulk
if I glanced at you too long.
You had raccoon eyeliner
& a dangling chain wallet
like a Hot Topic teen. In your
notebook, you wrote *where*
do I put this lust? because you
had a woman & still listened
for when I stepped out of the pool
at night. Back in the city,
over brunch, I said OK when you
told me you didn't identify
as a woman & I meant to ask
what pronouns you used.
I got lost in your swirled hair.
You invited me to a party
& arrived with a new woman
younger than us. I took a selfie

with your teacup dog. How many
women did you walk through
to reach me? You refused
to dance, but I would not leave
without joy, not after Orlando.
Out of tired politeness, I danced
with your date, who looked
up at me, submissive & intent.
Was it an audition? She said
polyamory worked for her,
Mormonism did not. My religion
was that I didn't share.
You kept drinking & I left early,
sober. The last time I saw you
it was raining at a protest rally.
We were strangers in the crowd.
You had no umbrella & I did
& neither of us could move.

Noli Me Tangere

the fields were scribbled on

or as blank as envelopes

*

to write about birds & not think *hunter*
not think *bright cage for two*

*

on the train, I slept in shuttering
light

through a bombed city returned
to its Baroque splendor

*

a friend once said *the body knows*

*

I played the ingénue

                                        the floating flower stalls
                                        lit through the rain
                                        like a beautiful alphabet

the azaleas were a parting gift

                                        as I drew a zipper
                                        shut across the continent—

                            *

            women are familiar with surrender
            & the appearance of it

Beach Date with End of the Alphabet Game

What is the deal with nightingales?
Orchids don't need perfume,
they've got their immaculate
beauty. You don't have
too many questions
as you arrange yourself
around me. I didn't want
to bring razors, but they
were all I could think of,
yikes. In my sunglassed sight
I scan the sand for signs
of my shell. A tumbleweed
rolls through. Hello
says the ocean, a kind of
reverse umbrella. This guy
is trying to stick to me
like velcro. Water,
clean this quiet. In conversation
I'm always waiting for
my xylophone cue. His mouth
is a yellowjacket, a blasted
wandering yellowjacket.
I wish the zoo would start
the stampede, the lions
carrying me aloft.

Night Ride

He left a bouquet of knots around the trees—
a different one each time he tied up the boat
along the pond. A few circles, a repeated knot
like a rose, a long branch wrapped like a latch.
Once the rain stopped, we rode the boat at night.
Frogs crept in the footlights along the path
& sent a chorus of *yeahs* ringing around the water.
We stopped rowing in the center. No stars,
no words: we took in what the moonlight gave to us
& it was enough. Like when I looked at him
as someone beautiful not meant for me.
I could not separate desire from catastrophe.
Shutting the doors by day, orbiting ecstatic
in the dancing darkness, silver streaking my hair.

Softer, Softest

Like a bandleader, one cardinal cuts through
the filigree trees. The poet rolls her shoulder,

wheels its notches, her muscles clicking out
as if flexing wings. For each tiny leaf & bud:

a pearl of rain. Last night, a man ripped his car
down the street & danced in his headlights

so the neighbors came out & screamed
into his trap song. Birds decorate the morning

trilling *is it you? is it me?* After too much caffeine,
the poet sweats, sways, & tries to write a line

about eternity. A bird possesses both a song
& a call. All day, she watched the glitter

travel across the pond like television snow.
A white pageant crowds her path

as she revives the spiraling feeling, the last time
a mouth ignited her like spring.

Invitation with Dirty Hands

as Frida Kahlo

In the blue house, my table examines
her hands & sets them on the floor.

Do the trees remember falling,
their branches snapping one by one

with their attendant flowers? I hear
fruit teething in wooden bowls.

The grave men walk with knives
up their sleeves. But I don't

blame them. I said *yes*. Stems refuse
& we break them. Happy skeleton,

dance with me: any part you want to play,
I will welcome you. I take care

of arranging fruit. My small beginnings—
do they lie buried like stones—

Blood in the dirt smears
my gleaming hands. Worms ribbon

into bodies below. Paradise
must have so many leaves

waving us forward in white sun.
Please arrive. Lie with me

among the weeds. I'm queen
for good. The marigolds

are latching into my bloodline.
Their soft throats crowd closer.

The Spring Forecast

Soon, the sea. On the city corner
        a tree asserts I *am every*
                shade of pink. Like the inside.
        Dresses as transparent
as watercolor. Doors flung open

              to receive gold arrows.
        (stringing the strings)
Skirts flare into bells. Hair
        like bougainvillea.
              Once, a stop sign

before the water. Once, he traced
        the arch of her foot. Women pack
              their illuminations
        in butterscotch leather trunks.
The sea rushes

              from the lighthouse. What bloom
        says no? Her hand
petaling open. What you
        would do for a pied-à-terre
              with tall windows & flower boxes.

A head full of leaves.

      Too many bows to tie

            & what of them? Pluck

      the bestsellers. Sandal

ready. A pointed foot,

            pointed feet. Come out, come out,

      my queens of color.

On the archipelago, you are

      almost new. Don't turn back:

            the women are walking again. They soak

in their many perfumes.

      (strings up) Soon, the island—

CODA

Pandemic Spring

Golden Gate Park rises before me. I follow different paths because this is no time for order. What's new is the greater quiet, as if the world is echoing me: a tentative glance, no touching. Along the secret lake, I linger under a cherry tree in full blossom, *as is my ancestral right*, something my Ohio friend once said to me about hunting in Virginia. When the petals fall like snow, I think *all my karaoke dreams*. One male mallard duck chases another who chases another. Is this about love? Maybe the hidden female wants to be alone. A slow spring. Loosening my mermaid hair. A siren splits the birdsong. Hours of falling & listening. I've given up coffee to lighten my heart, but a knot remains. The cat taps my ankle to ask for a pet, but not a hug, never a hug. Years ago, after the separation, I couldn't sense anything until the spring, when a woman's song broke over me. The days are unspeakable. Color becomes a feeling: a spray of shocked orange poppies, tiny golden creeping buttercups, serene Chinese hibiscus. A great blue heron steps out of the grass. I wear pale pink to bloom—a pastel queen, soft sight. There is a gentleness that returns once you let go of love's disappointment. A fleeting expanse in the compressed day. When only the birds are with me, I embrace a redwood tree, breathing it in. Dear ancestor: I am always rapidly departing, forgive me. To live, I want to be known & loved, the two together, inseparable.

Notes

"Private Collection" refers to the following artworks: Vija Celmins' *Untitled (Ocean)*, Gerhard Richter's *Lesende (Reader)*, and Johannes Vermeer's *Young Woman with a Water Pitcher* (this painting also inspired "Vermeer at the Metropolitan Museum of Art"). Located on the Acropolis of Athens, the Erechtheion is an ancient Greek temple whose Porch of the Maidens featured six draped women figures (caryatids) as supporting columns. Today, the onsite caryatids are replicas and five originals are housed in the Acropolis Museum. Lord Elgin removed another caryatid from the Acropolis site in the early 1800s and it remains part of the Elgin Marbles at the British Museum.

"Department of the Interior" borrows the italicized line from "The Fish" by Elizabeth Bishop.

The film referenced in "To Yellow" is *Great Expectations* (1996) directed by Alfonso Cuarón.

"Women After Midnight" refers to the Christian Marclay's video installation *The Clock*, which is comprised of film clips mentioning or showing the time, ordered and organized in an exact 24-hour period.

"White Rabbit" refers to *Then She Fell*, an immersive theater experience that ran in Brooklyn from 2012 to 2020. It was based on Lewis Carroll's *Alice's Adventures in Wonderland* and other works and the real Alice Liddell.

"All Beyoncés and Lucy Lius": The title borrows a lyric from "Hey Ya" by OutKast and the poem borrows a lyric from "Independent Women Part I" by Destiny's Child, a song featured in the film adaptation *Charlie's Angels* (2000). "Like a G6" by Far East Movement, The Cataracs, and Dev was the first single by Asian American artists to hit number one on the *Billboard* Hot 100.

"Exit Strategist" borrows its form from "Flight" by Suji Kwock Kim.

"Pride Month" borrows a line from "No Miracle, No Act of God" by Jacques Rancourt. In the LGBTQ+ community, the phrase "wife" can used for one's partner, reflecting the years prior to legal same-sex marriage.

"The Ocean Will Take Us One Day" was written in fall 2016, concurrent with the Dakota Access Pipeline protests, a supermoon, and the US presidential election.

"Invitation with Three Colors" refers to the performance piece *Rest Energy* by Marina Abramović and Ulay.

"Pandemic Spring" was written in spring 2020. The song referenced is "Lazuli" by Beach House.

A longer series of Frida Kahlo poems appears in my chapbook *RARE BIRDS* (Diode Editions, 2017).

Acknowledgments

My sincere thanks to the readers and editors of the publications in which some of these poems appeared in their first forms, sometimes under alternate titles:

The Adroit Journal: "Epithalamium"

American Poetry Review: "Invitation with Three Colors"

The Collagist: "The Fall Forecast"

The Cortland Review: "Department of the Interior," "Memorial Day Weekend"

Crazyhorse: "The Spring Forecast"

Diode: "Women After Midnight"

Drunken Boat: "Dear Frida"

Fairy Tale Review: "Winter Pineapple with Sea"

Foglifter: "Night Ride"

Gulf Coast: "The Summer Forecast"

The Los Angeles Review: "Monolids"

Kenyon Review: "All Beyoncés & Lucy Lius," "The Ocean Will Take Us One Day," "Pride Month"

Massachusetts Review: "My Therapist Asks If I Would Be Happier If I Were Straight"

Nashville Review: "Vermeer at the Metropolitan Museum of Art"

New England Review: "The Winter Forecast"

The New Republic: "For the Living in the New World"

Ninth Letter Online: "White Rabbit"

The Normal School: "Perennials"

The Offing: "The Allergy Test," "Beach Date with End of the Alphabet Game," "Pursuit"

Poetry Northwest: "Pandemic Spring," "Private Collection," "Weather Advisory"

Sixth Finch: "Courtship," "To Yellow"

Southern Humanities Review: "Invitation with Dirty Hands"

Sycamore Review: "Noli Me Tangere"

Vinyl: "Exit Strategist"

wildness: "Watch Hill"

Waxwing: "Refrain," "Walking Across Fire Island"

"The Spring Forecast" was selected for a Pushcart Prize in the 2017 *Pushcart Prize XLI* anthology. "Perennials" won the 2014 Normal Prize for poetry. "All Beyoncés & Lucy Lius" and "The Ocean Will Take Us One Day" were reprinted in *They Rise Like A Wave: An Anthology of Asian American Women Poets* (White Pine Press). "Interlude" was published in *Written Here: The Community of Writers Poetry Review 2016*.

This book is the culmination of a long journey. Thank you and highest love to my family for your encouragement, love, and support over the years.

My gratitude to MacDowell and Star studio for my first residency, supported by the 2017 MacDowell Poetry Fellowship. Thank you to Headlands Center for the Arts, I-Park Foundation, Fire Island National Seashore, SPACE, and the Brown-Handler Writer's Residency/San Francisco Public Library for time and space to create. Thank you to Kenyon Review Writers Workshop, Fine Arts Work Center, Palm Beach Poetry Festival, New York State Summer Writers Institute, Napa Valley Writers Conference, Kearny Street Workshop's Interdisciplinary Writers Lab, Community of Writers, and RADAR/San Francisco Public Library for your support and community.

Thank you to the creative writing programs and English departments at the Ohio State University, University of California at Berkeley, and Oxford University. My gratitude to the many teachers whose guidance has shaped me.

My love and appreciation to my mentor Kathy Fagan Grandinetti for your kindness and brilliance—you are forever crowned. Thank you to my writing and literature professors Jennifer Schlueter, Henri Cole, and Brenda Brueggemann for your expanse.

I am grateful to Mary Szybist, David Baker, Aracelis Girmay, Don Mee Choi, Srikanth Reddy, Gabrielle Calvocoressi, and Chinaka Hodge for your workshop insights and invaluable feedback. Many thanks to Chloe Honum, Tracy K. Smith, Emily Rosko, and Eduardo C. Corral for your recognition and encouragement.

I have so much love and joy for Raena Shirali, Mikko Harvey, Janelle DolRayne, Michael Marberry, Allison Pitinii Davis, and Nick White—thank you for your wisdom, friendship, and support. Special thanks and love to Jacques Rancourt for reading this manuscript so carefully and caring for its vision.

Thank you to so many incredible artists and writers of color for our conversations and your work. Ecstatic love to my Kundiman family, especially Sarah Gambito, Joseph Legaspi, Oliver de la Paz, Cathy Linh Che, Brynn Saito, Jason Bayani, Muriel Leung, Monica Sok, Sally Wen Mao, Dan Lau, Truong Tran, Michelle Lin, Kazumi Chin, Paul Tran, Ploi Pirapokin, Emily Yamauchi, Jay Deshpande, and Kenji Liu. Much appreciation to the staff, interns, volunteers, and board members over the years for your commitment and care.

Special thanks to Aay Preston-Myint, Holly Blake, and Damon Little at Headlands Center for the Arts for supporting and feeding local artists through a pandemic. Forever love to the final HCA affiliate artist cohort and the artists and writers I encountered there over three years, especially Hazel White and Connie Zheng. Building 960 forever.

Thank you to so many bright lights in community: Patty Paine, Keetje Kuipers, Carly Jo Miller, Carl Phillips, Tiana Clark, Michael Dhyne, Cate Lycurgus, Lisa Hiton, Khaty Xiong, Margaree Little, Amanda Moore, Nathan Lipps, R. Zamora Linmark, Laura Mullen, John Murillo, Jenny Han, Kate Calimquim, and Lucy Shon-Santana, among others. For professional support, leadership, and care, thank you to UCSF legend Brenda Gee.

Big love to my Ohio State community: Nathan Thomas, Kristen Grayewski, Nina Yun, David Winter, J. Brendan Shaw, Lo Kwa Mei-En, Lauren Clay Barret, Rebecca Turkewitz, and Cait Weiss Orcutt. Thank you to Eddie Singleton and Jonathan Buehl for your teaching mentorship and to Tammy Carl and Kelli Fickle for your kind support of the MFA program.

Many thanks to KMA Sullivan and Stevie Edwards at YesYes Books for believing in the work and for your insights, time, and care for this book during a pandemic. Thank you to Alban Fischer for honoring my book with the cover of my dreams. Thank you to Cole Hildebrand, Jill Kolongowski, and the rest of the YesYes team for all that you do to support your authors.

A bouquet of thanks to Mary Szybist, Ocean Vuong, Keetje Kuipers, and Diana Khoi Nguyen for introducing my book into the world with your generous words—you light the way. Thank you to my publicist Jennifer Huang at the Shipman Agency for your brilliant and thoughtful partnership.

For artistic freedom and joy, eternal love to Michelle Kwan, Madonna, Frida Kahlo, Tegan & Sara, Tori Amos, and BTS.

My deepest gratitude to my ancestors and elders and to the past and present generations of Asian American poets and writers—for all that you created, lived through, and built.

And lastly, sweetest love to my cats Melody and Charlotte for your love and patience from New York to San Francisco, and all of the stops along our journey.

Also from YesYes Books

FICTION

Girls Like Me by Nina Packebush

Three Queerdos and a Baby by Nina Packebush

WRITING RESOURCES

Gathering Voices: Creating a Community-Based Poetry Workshop by Marty McConnell

FULL-LENGTH COLLECTIONS

Ugly Music by Diannely Antigua

Gutter by Lauren Brazeal

What Runs Over by Kayleb Rae Candrilli

This, Sisyphus by Brandon Courtney

Salt Body Shimmer by Aricka Foreman

Forever War by Kate Gaskin

Ceremony of Sand by Rodney Gomez

Undoll by Tanya Grae

Loudest When Startled by Lukas Ray Hall

Everything Breaking / For Good by Matt Hart

Sons of Achilles by Nabila Lovelace

Landscape with Sex and Violence by Lynn Melnick

Refusenik by Lynn Melnick

GOOD MORNING AMERICA I AM HUNGRY AND ON FIRE by jamie mortara

Stay by Tanya Olson

a falling knife has no handle by Emily O'Neill

To Love An Island by Ana Portnoy Brimmer

RECENT CHAPBOOK COLLECTIONS

21982320540242

CPSIA information can be obtained
at www.ICGtesting.com
Printed in the USA
LVHW080925220922
728951LV00014B/533

9 781936 919895